Hooked on Limericks

A Collection of Crochet Limericks

by
Just Limericks

Table of Contents

Welcome to "Hooked on Limericks", a collection of whimsical limericks about the craft of crochet. In these pages, you'll find limericks about crocheters of all skill levels, from beginners to experts, and the triumphs and tribulations they experience in their craft.

Whether you're a seasoned crocheter or new to the art, we hope these limericks will bring a smile to your face and inspire you to pick up your hook and yarn. So sit back, relax, and enjoy the amusing and charming world of crochet through the power of limericks!

There was a young lady who loved to crochet
She crocheted all night and crocheted all day
She made a scarf for her cat
A hat for her rat
And a cozy for her teapot, by the way

The Crocheted Scarf: A Rainbow of Colors

In the chilly month of December,
A young woman named Amber,
Picked up a crochet hook,
And took a determined look,
To make a scarf that would never be a slumber.

She started with a chain of just ten,
And worked her way through again and again,
Adding stitches and rows,
And all sorts of crochet pros,
To create a scarf that was longer than ten.

She crocheted through the days and the nights,
And occasionally paused for a few bites,
Of cookies and tea,
And maybe some brie,
As she worked on her scarf with all her might.

Finally, after weeks of work,
She completed the scarf with a final jerk,
And held it up to the light,
A rainbow of colors, so bright,
A masterpiece she was truly able to perk.

So if you see her walking around,
With her scarf so beautifully wound,
Stop her and ask,
For the secret to her task,
And maybe she'll teach you to crochet, unbound.

Stitching Serenity: A Crochet Journey

In Stitching Serenity, we embark
On a crochet journey, so let's start
With a hook and some yarn
We'll make something darn
And create a masterpiece with heart

We'll stitch and we'll purl with delight
As our fingers work magic in flight
And when we're all done
We'll have lots of fun
Showing off our creations so bright

So come along on this crochet ride
With Stitching Serenity as your guide
We'll create something new
With every stitch we pursue
And our love for crochet will never subside.

As she sits down with yarn and hook,
Her mind begins to calm and unhook.
The world fades away,
As her hands start to play,
And her stitches create a new look.

With each loop and twist of her wrist,
A sense of accomplishment exists.
Each stitch a small win,
A journey to begin,
As she creates something from a mere list.

The colors she chooses to blend,
On her hook, they start to transcend.
A work of art forms,
As the yarn takes on forms,
And a sense of joy starts to extend.

So Stitching Serenity begins,
A crochet journey that never ends.
With yarn and hook in hand,
She'll create something grand,
As she smiles and her heart starts to mend.

The Crochet Chronicles:
One Hook, Countless Possibilities

The Crochet Chronicles tell of a tale
Of a hook and a ball of yarn without fail
One day they met and decided to mate
And create something that would be truly great

They worked together, stitch by stitch
And created something without a glitch
A scarf, a hat, a cozy blanket
Each project they made was a complete hit

The hook and the yarn, they were quite a pair
They made crochet seem easy and fair
With each project they completed with ease
They proved that anyone can crochet with breeze

As they continued their crochet journey
They met many others who loved this artistry
Together they shared tips, tricks, and patterns
And created things that were nothing short of a lantern

The Crochet Chronicles have just begun
There's still so much to learn and fun to be won
With each stitch and every row they take
The possibilities for creation are simply infinite

She searched for a project to try,
A new stitch to catch her eye.
A blanket or a hat,
Or maybe a cute cat,
The possibilities made her sigh.

She decided on a new scarf to make,
A challenge she was eager to take.
The pattern was tricky,
But she wasn't picky,
And she worked on it until daybreak.

Her hook moved quick as lightning,
Her fingers were busy and exciting.
With every new row,
Her scarf seemed to glow,
Her talent was truly inviting.

As she finished her work with delight,
She wrapped the scarf around her tight.
The colors were bright,
The scarf was just right,
And it made her feel quite alright.

She went out to show off her creation,
Walking around with such elation.
People stopped and stared,
And many people cared,
For her scarf was a true sensation.

From that day on, she crocheted with glee,
Making things for all to see.
Her hook was her friend,
And she'd never let it end,
For crochet was her true destiny.

Knotting and Yarning: A Crochet Memoir

In Knotting and Yarning, our hero
Found joy in each crocheting zero
With hooks and with yarn
A new scarf was born
And soon became quite the hero

She crocheted in colors so bright
With hooks that were shiny and light
The yarn she would spin
Into hats and mittens
And blankets that kept folks warm at night

Her stitches were often askew
But that just made her talent shine through
For each piece she made
Was unique in its way
And brought joy to those who knew

One day she tried something quite new
A pattern she'd never pursue
It took quite some time
But when it was done
It was fit for a king or queen, too

She continued to crochet with glee
Through winter, spring, summer, and fall with glee
With each stitch and turn
Her passion would burn
For the art of crochet, you see

Now she's a crocheting sensation
Known in every crocheting nation
For her hooks and yarn
Have made her a star
In the world of crocheting creation

The Witty Yarns of a Crochet Connoisseur: A Silly Memoir

Once upon a time, a crochet enthusiast
Decided to take on a new crochet quest
She rummaged through her stash
To find yarn with a flash
And chose a neon pink to make a funky vest

With her trusty hook, she started to crochet
Row after row, she worked her way
But her stitch count was wrong
It was too short all along
So she frogged it and started again the next day

This time, she was determined to succeed
Her fingers worked fast, she picked up speed
But she forgot to count once more
And ended up with twenty-three
Too many or too few, she couldn't quite read

She ripped it out once again, feeling vexed
But she refused to give up on this project
She watched a YouTube tutorial
To make sure she didn't mess up the tutorial
But the cat stepped on her work, leaving her perplexed

She sighed and picked up her hook once more
She had never been defeated before
She counted her stitches carefully
To make sure she didn't do it sloppily
And finally, she completed the vest she adored

She wore it proudly and showed it off with flair
Everyone complimented her on her crochet affair
She was pleased with the final result
And grateful for the lessons she was taught
Crochet was her passion, and she loved it beyond
compare

From Yarn to Scarf: A Crochet Adventure

With hook in hand, she starts with a loop
And pulls the yarn with a swoop
She's on a mission, not to be deterred
For making a scarf, she's undeterred
Her stitches are neat, not a single group

Her hands work fast, she's a crocheting pro
In every stitch, she has to go
She's making a scarf, oh so fine
One that will surely stand the test of time
Her confidence grows, she's in the flow

With each stitch, she's making progress
It's looking good, she must confess
But wait, what's this? Oh no, a mistake
She must rip it out, for goodness sake
Her patience is tested, but she won't regress

Back to the start, but she's not disheartened
Her hook is moving, she's not to be pardoned
The yarn is flying, her fingers nimble
She's crocheting fast, like a stitchin' thimble
Her determination, she has hardened

At last, the scarf is finally done
A masterpiece, she has won
She tries it on, it's snug and warm
This crochet adventure, she'll always adorn
A proud achievement, her heart has spun

The Sweater Saga: A Crochet Tale

In her chair, she sat down to crochet
A sweater she'd wear every day
She picked out some yarn
And then she'd darn
And stitch till it was just her way

She worked and worked on every stitch
To make sure it would be a perfect fit
She crocheted and crocheted
And almost strayed
But kept going, not wanting to quit

At last, she finished the first sleeve
It was the right size, you'd believe
But when she went to attach
It had a major mismatch
And she realized she'd have to retrieve

So she ripped it out and started again
Working on every stitch, time and again
She'd take it apart
And rework it, smart
Until the sweater was perfect, my friend

Now she wears it with pride every day
Her sweater, her crochet display
And when people ask where
She just points and shares
"It's a one-of-a-kind, what can I say?"

The Crochet Crusader

The Crochet Crusader was her name,
In her hands, every yarn looked the same,
She would hook and loop,
Until she had a cozy soup,
That would keep her warm like a burning flame.

With every stitch, she grew more confident,
Her creations were becoming quite prominent,
A scarf, a hat, even a shawl,
She could crochet them all,
And her friends and family were quite content.

But then one day, she had a new idea,
A crochet masterpiece that would bring her cheer,
A giant yarn sculpture,
Of a magical creature,
And she set to work with enthusiasm and cheer.

For days and nights, she crocheted with glee,
Until finally, the creature was complete and free,
It was a wondrous sight,
With colors so bright,
And it brought a smile to everyone she could see.

From then on, the Crochet Crusader was renowned,
Her creations were famous, all over town,
She would crochet every day,
In every possible way,
And her love for yarn would never, ever drown.

Teaching Crochet to a Newbie

There once was a teacher of crochet
Who met a young newbie one day
She said with a smile,
"I'll teach you awhile,
And soon you'll be crocheting away."

She showed her the chain stitch with pride
And watched as the newbie complied
Then double and single
And how to untangle
And all the tricks she could provide

The newbie was eager to learn
But sometimes her stitches would turn
The teacher would say,
"Don't worry, okay,
Just rip it out and give it a burn."

As time went on, the newbie improved
Her stitches were no longer so skewed
She crocheted with glee
And soon she could see
A scarf and a hat in her groove

Then one day, the teacher fell ill
And couldn't teach crochet with her skill
But the newbie said, "Wait,
I'll crochet you a cape,
And with this, you'll get better still."

So she picked up her hook and some yarn
And crocheted the cape without harm
And when it was done,
She gave it to the one
Who taught her to crochet on her farm.

And now the two of them crochet
Together, day after day
The teacher and newbie
A duo so groovy
In their own crocheting way.

The Great Yarn Untangling

There was a crocheter so bold,
Their yarn stash was getting quite old.
In the corner it sat,
All tangled and flat,
Like a cat that was caught in a hold.

The crocheter, they tried to begin,
To untangle the yarn with a grin.
They pulled and they tugged,
But the yarn wouldn't budge,
And the situation started to spin.

The yarn was a tangled mess,
And the crocheter started to stress.
They tried every trick,
But the yarn wouldn't flick,
And they thought they might need a caress.

With a deep breath and a sigh,
The crocheter gave it another try.
They pulled and they teased,
And they even said please,
But the yarn still wouldn't comply.

Finally, after hours of toil,
And enough coffee to make their blood boil,
The yarn was set free,
And the crocheter could see,
Their project no longer in turmoil.

So if you're a crocheter, beware,
Of the tangled yarn's devilish stare.
But with patience and pluck,
And some good luck,
You can untangle your yarn with great care.

The Struggle of Trying
a New Crochet Stitch

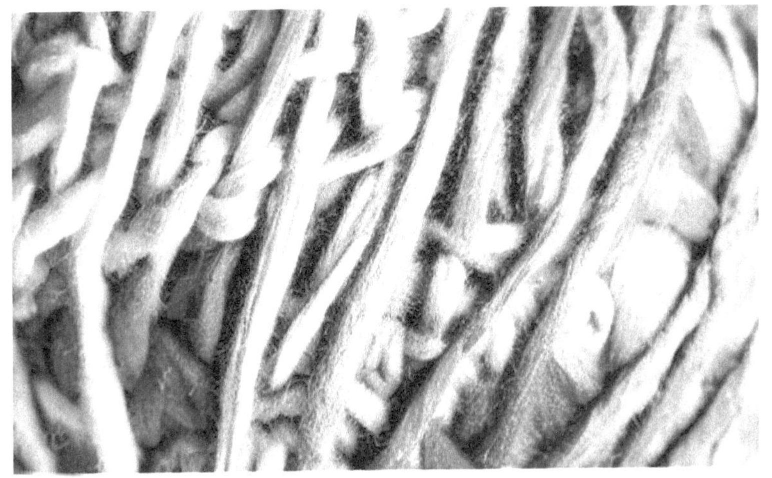

Trying a new stitch, with much trepidation
She picked up the hook and yarn of sensation
Her first few attempts looked like a mess
She couldn't quite get it, no matter how she'd address
The pattern instructions seemed like pure incantation

She looked at the picture, then back at the book
It seemed like a foreign language, some kind of
crocheting rook
Her fingers fumbled, the yarn slipped
This new stitch had her feeling whipped
But still she persevered, with her hook she shook

As the hours passed, her patience was thinning
The frustration she felt was beginning
Her project still looked like a sorry sight
But she knew she couldn't give up the fight
So she kept on hooking, her fingers spinning

Finally, she got the hang of the new stitch
Her confidence grew, no longer feeling like such a
glitch
With each row, her tension was better
She could crochet this stitch, like a pro letter by letter
And now she was really itching to stitch!

She thought she knew all the stitches,
But one day, she found new riches.
A pattern she found, it was divine,
But this new stitch made her lose her mind.
She tried and tried, but nothing seemed to click.

She watched a tutorial, and read a book,
But nothing helped, she couldn't get the hook
To make the stitch as it should be,
It was driving her crazy, as you can see.
She was determined, though, to master this trick.

She finally got it, after many tries,
She let out a shout, and wiped her eyes.
She couldn't believe she had made it work,
And now she could finally finish her work.
It was a struggle, but she didn't give up so quick.

With her new stitch, she feels so alive,
Her crochet projects now thrive.
She's conquered this challenge, and it's plain to see,
That learning new stitches is the key.
To taking her crochet game to the next level and
thrive.

Hooked on Crochet: A Yarn of Laughter

There once was a crocheter so skilled,
Whose yarn stash could never be filled.
With a hook in each hand,
And a plan oh so grand,
She crocheted a scarf that thrilled.

But then she got lost in the skeins,
And her hook got caught in the reins.
The yarn began to unwind,
Leaving her in a bind,
As she struggled to untangle the pains.

Her cat sat and watched with great glee,
As she fought with the tangled debris.
But the crocheter was smart,
And she knew in her heart,
That the yarn could be tamed, you see.

So she took a deep breath and began,
To unravel the yarn with her hands.
She worked on each knot,
And soon she had caught,
The loose threads and tangled strands.

And when the yarn was all free,
She crocheted with such great glee.
A scarf so soft and so warm,
That kept her safe from the storm,
And left her feeling oh so carefree.

The Lost Crochet Hook

Amidst a sea of yarn so bright,
She crocheted with all her might,
Until she noticed with chagrin,
Her hook was lost, it wasn't in.
She looked around, beneath her seat,

She searched her yarn, and all beneath,
High and low, without much relief,
But her hook just wouldn't show,
Her mood turned sour, her pace grew slow,
Without her hook, she felt incomplete.

She sighed and groaned, she felt so stuck,
She needed her hook, without any luck,
But then she had a brilliant thought,
A new hook she could have bought,
To save her from her crocheting rut.

She ran to the store, she ran with glee,
And picked a hook, size 3.5mm, you see,
She paid the price, she left the place,
And went back home, at a quicker pace,
Eager to continue her crochet spree.

And from that day, she learned her lesson,
To keep a spare hook, was her confession.
Now she crochets with ease and glee,
With a spare hook for emergency.
Never again will she lose her possession.

The Big Finish: A Crochet Tale

There once was a crocheter with style
Whose projects were sure to beguile
She worked through the night
With yarn soft and bright
Her craft room a colorful pile

She made blankets, hats, scarves, and more
With stitches so tight, not a bore
Her friends all would ask
For a new crochet task
And they'd marvel at all she'd explore

One day she decided to start
A project that would test her heart
She crocheted with glee
And oh how it would be
Her masterpiece, a true work of art

For weeks she would stitch and she'd sew
Through highs and through lows, don't you know
Her fingers would ache
Her eyes would just quake
But she'd never let her work go

At last, the big finish was nigh
Her project was done, oh my, oh my
She held it up high
And let out a sigh
Her heart soared, she felt she could fly

With yarn in her hand, she beamed bright
Her friends all admired her sight
She laughed and she twirled
Her project unfurled
It was perfect, oh what a delight

Now the crocheter had achieved her goal
Her crochet prowess had taken its toll
She knew she was blessed
Her talent, the best
And her projects, they would never grow old.

The Tale of the Tangled Yarn

There once was a crocheter so fine,
Whose skills were second to none, divine.
But one day, she found,
A ball of yarn so wound,
It left her in a mess, tangled and confined.

She tried and tried to untangle the mess,
But the yarn was stubborn, causing much distress.
She pulled and she tugged,
But the knot wouldn't budge,
She was close to giving up, nothing left to address.

She took a deep breath, and thought it through,
She had to find a way to see it through.
She started slow, inch by inch,
And soon the tangle was in a cinch,
With her skills, she knew just what to do.

She finally emerged victorious from the fray,
A beautiful scarf was ready to display.
With patience and care,
She conquered the snare,
And now she's known as the yarn whisperer, they say.

So if you're ever in a tangle, don't fret,
Just take your time and don't be upset.
With skill and determination,
You can conquer any situation,
And create something beautiful, you won't regret.

The Unraveling Scarf

Once there was a crocheter, so keen,
Who started a project with a skein,
But as she worked on her scarf,
She realized with a sharp laugh,
That it was coming apart at the seam!

She tugged at the yarn with great care,
Trying to keep her cool and not swear,
She took a deep breath,
And pondered her death,
For the scarf was a tangled nightmare!

She tried to unravel the mess,
But it only seemed to grow and suppress,
She wished for a miracle,
Or a fairy with a spectacle,
To fix the mistake and bring success.

But then she had an idea so bold,
To cut the yarn and be brave and so cold,
She snipped it with scissors,
And then with a blizzard,
She tied the ends into a knot, so bold.

And just like that, the scarf was saved,
And the crocheter was so overjoyed, she raved,
She put it on with glee,
And danced in the street, so free,
With her new scarf, she felt so brave!

From Tangled to Terrific:
A Crochet Journey

With a hook and yarn, she began,
But her work was far from a plan,
Her stitches were tight,
Her tension was a fright,
Until she mastered crochet by hand.

She tried to crochet with grace,
Her work was a tangled disgrace.
The tension was off,
And her stitches, a scoff,
Until she learned to crochet with pace.

When she first picked up hook and string,
Her hopes to crochet took a fling.
But try as she might,
Her work wasn't quite right,
Her stitches too loose or too cling.

When she tried to crochet with ease,
Her work was a jumbled unease.
The tension was off,
And her stitches, a scoff,
Until she learned to crochet with breeze.

She watched videos to her delight,
And read books late into the night.
She tried and she tried,
And her skills did abide,
Until her crochet was a true sight.

Now she creates with such great speed,
And her projects have such lovely breed.
Her stitches so neat,
Her tension a treat,
And her work is what many folks need.

With each project, her confidence grew,
She tried new stitches, and she knew
That with time and with care,
She could make anything rare,
Her crochet skills became quite the coup.

She tackled each pattern with glee,
And her hooks moved with such symmetry,
No longer a novice,
She felt quite accomplished,
Her crochet dreams now a reality.

Her friends and family were amazed,
By the things she could now create,
They begged for her skill,
And asked for their fill,
Of her beautiful crochet art to display.

So she started her own little shop,
And her crochet skills, she didn't stop,
Her customers all knew,
That she had something new,
And her business soon became a top pop.

The Frustrated Crocheter

There once was a crocheter so fine
Whose project just wouldn't align
With a hook in their hand
And yarn all unplanned
They tossed it away in a bind.

But then they saw it in their dreams
Their project, all perfect, it seems
With a renewed sensc of zeal
They picked up their steel
And crocheted away, so extreme.

They counted their stitches with care
And checked their gauge, a meticulous affair
The pattern was followed
No mistake was swallowed
And their work, it started to flare.

With a newfound patience in tow
The crocheter's frustration did go
And the project was done
All shiny and spun
A beautiful sight to bestow.

Now the crocheter knows what to do
When their project goes askew
Take a deep breath and try
And before you know, by and by
Your work will be stunning, it's true.

The Granny Square Scandal

In the yarn store, she found a great skein
And decided to make a granny square chain.
She started to crochet,
In her own special way,
But soon her project was causing her pain.

Her squares were all different in size,
And her colors didn't match up to her eyes.
She couldn't figure out,
What she was doing wrong without a doubt,
And her frustration began to rise.

She tried to unravel and start again,
But she kept making the same old sin.
Her tension was off,
And her patience, a scoff,
Until she found a solution in the end.

She watched a tutorial online,
And suddenly, everything became fine.
Her squares were now neat,
And her colors, a treat,
And her project was finally divine.

With each square, her confidence grew,
And soon her project was nearly through.
She showed it off with pride,
And her friends all sighed,
At the beautiful blanket she had made anew.

From that day on, she learned to take care,
And make sure her tension was always fair.
She never gave up,
And her crochet, she loved,
And her projects were always a hit everywhere.

The Crochet Project Disaster

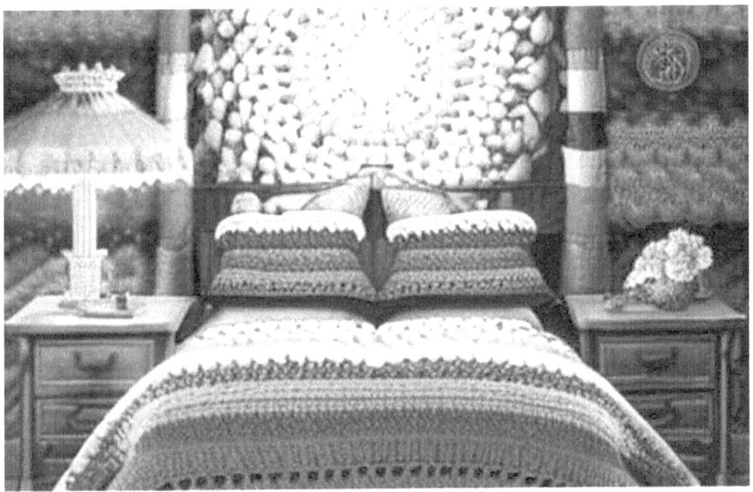

A woman began a crochet scheme,
To make a blanket that was supreme.
She chose the yarn and the hook,
And started with a cheerful look,
But soon things were not as they seemed.

She crocheted and crocheted with care,
But found her stitches were beyond repair.
The blanket grew too wide,
And she couldn't seem to hide,
The mess that she had created there.

She tried to unravel the whole thing,
But her hook got caught in the string.
She pulled and she tugged,
But the yarn just shrugged,
And the project turned into a big fling.

She got tangled up in the skeins,
And the yarn wrapped around her like chains.
She stumbled and fell,
In a mess that looked like hell,
But she couldn't stop laughing from the pains.

In the end, she decided to quit,
And leave the blanket as it is unfit.
She hung it up on the wall,
As a reminder to all,
That sometimes crochet is a funny misfit

www.justlimericks.com

www.ingramcontent.com/pod-product-compliance
Lightning Source LLC
Chambersburg PA
CBHW061400160726
47995CB00001B/402